The First Family of
HOPE

The OBAMAS

Barack

Michelle

Malia

Sasha

The Obama Family Tree

Obama Mania

Michelle

Hal Marcovitz

Mason Crest Publishers

Produced by 21st Century Publishing and Communications, Inc.

MASON CREST PUBLISHERS INC.
370 Reed Road
Broomall, Pennsylvania 19008
(866) MCP-BOOK (toll free)
www.masoncrest.com

Printed in the United States of America.

First Printing

9 8 7 6 5 4 3 2 1

Library of Congress Cataloging-in-Publication Data

Marcovitz, Hal.
  Michelle / Hal Marcovitz.
    p. cm. — (The Obamas : first family of hope)
  ISBN 978-1-4222-1478-7 (hardcover : alk. paper)
  ISBN 978-1-4222-1485-5 (pbk. : alk. paper)
  1. Obama, Michelle, 1964–   —Juvenile literature. 2. Presidents' spouses—United States—Biography—Juvenile literature. 3. Legislators' spouses—United States—Biography—Juvenile literature. 4. African American women lawyers—Illinois—Chicago—Biography—Juvenile literature. 5. Chicago (Ill.)—Biography—Juvenile literature I. Title.
E909.O24M37 2009
973.932092—dc22
[B]   2009000139

Publisher's notes:
All quotations in this book come from original sources, and contain the spelling and grammatical inconsistencies of the original text.

The Web sites mentioned in this book were active at the time of publication. The publisher is not responsible for Web sites that have changed their addresses or discontinued operation since the date of publication. The publisher will review and update the Web site addresses each time the book is reprinted.

Contents

Introduction

On November 4, 2008, Barack Obama made history—he was the first black American to be elected president of the United States. The Obama family—Barack, wife Michelle, and daughters Malia and Sasha, became the first African-American first family.

THE FIRST FAMILY OF HOPE

The stories of the Obamas are fascinating and uniquely American. The six books in this series take you center stage and behind the scenes, with crafted and insightful storytelling, as well as hundreds of dynamic and telling photographs. Discover six unique inside perspectives on the Obama family's extraordinary journey and the Obama mania that surrounds it.

WHERE IT ALL BEGAN

Many generations ago, in the late 1600s, Barack's mother's ancestors arrived in colonial America as white emigrants from Europe, while his father's ancestors lived in villages in Kenya, Africa. Michelle's ancestors were shipped from Africa to America as slaves.

Generations later, Barack, son of a black father and a white mother, spent his childhood in Hawaii and Indonesia; while Michelle, a descendant of slaves, was growing up in Chicago. Later they both graduated from Harvard Law School, got married, and became proud parents of two beautiful daughters. Barack tackled injustice as a community organizer in Chicago, later entered politics, and was elected to the U.S. Senate.

"THE AUDACITY OF HOPE"

In 2004, at the Democratic National Convention, Barack Obama made an electrifying keynote speech, "The Audacity of Hope." He asked Americans to find unity in diversity and hope in the future. His message resonated with the attendees and millions of television viewers. Barack was catapulted from obscurity into the spotlight, and the Obama phenomenon had begun.

"YES WE CAN!"

On February 10, 2007, Barack announced his candidacy for the office of president of the United States. His family and legions of volunteers all over the country campaigned vigorously for him, and nearly two years later, the Obama family stood proudly in front of more than 240,000 supporters who gathered to hear Barack's victory speech. Tears streamed down the

The Obamas (left to right) Malia, Michelle, Sasha, and Barack, wave to their devoted fans. Barack has energized millions of people in the United States and around the world with his message of unity and hope.

faces of people who believed this was nothing short of a miracle. Tens of millions of television viewers worldwide watched and listened with a renewed sense of hope as President-elect Obama proclaimed:

> **❝This victory is yours. . . . If there is anyone out there who still doubts that America is a place where all things are possible; who still wonders if the dream of our founders is alive in our time; who still questions the power of our democracy, tonight is your answer. ❞**

OBAMA FAMILY TIMELINE

1600s to 1700s
Barack Obama's mother's ancestors immigrate to the American colonies from Europe.

1936
Barack Obama, Sr., Barack's father, is born in a small village in Kenya, Africa.

1964
Barack's parents, Barack Obama, Sr. and Ann Dunham are divorced.

1700s to 1800s
Michelle Robinson Obama's ancestors arrive in the American colonies as slaves.

1937
Michelle's mother, Marian Shields, is born.

1967
Barack's mother marries Lolo Soetoro and moves the family to Soetoro's home country, Indonesia.

1850s
Michelle's great-great grandfather is born a slave in South Carolina.

1942
Barack's mother, Ann Dunham, is born in Kansas.

1971
Barack returns to Hawaii and lives with his grandparents.

1600   **1900**   **1950**   **1982**

1912
Michelle's grandfather, Fraser Robinson Jr., is born.

1959
Barack Obama, Sr. comes to America as a student.

1979
Barack graduates from high school and enrolls in Occidental College in Los Angeles, California.

1918
Barack's grandfather, Stanley Dunham, is born.

February 21, 1961
Barack Obama, Sr. and Ann Dunham are married.

1922
Barack's grandmother, Madelyn Payne, is born.

August 4, 1961
Barack is born in Honolulu, Hawaii.

1981
Barack transfers to Columbia University in New York City.

1935
Michelle's father, Fraser Robinson III, is born.

January 17, 1964
Michelle is born in Chicago, Illinois.

1982
Barack's father dies in Kenya, Africa.

1988
Michelle graduates from Harvard Law School.

1988
Barack enters Harvard Law School.

1990
Barack is elected president of the *Harvard Law Review*.

1991
Barack graduates from Harvard Law School.

1995
Barack's first book, *Dreams from My Father*, is published.

1998
Barack and Michelle's first daughter, Malia, is born.

2001
Barack and Michelle's second daughter, Sasha, is born.

July 2004
Barack delivers keynote speech at Democratic National Convention.

November 2, 2008
Barack's grandmother dies in Hawaii.

November 4, 2008
Barack is elected the first African-American president of the United States.

January 20, 2009
Barack is sworn in as the 44th president of the United States.

1983   1995   2006   2009

1988
Barack visits his relatives in Kenya, Africa.

1985
Michelle graduates from Princeton University.

1985
Barack moves to Chicago, Illinois, to work as a community organizer.

1983
Barack graduates from Columbia University.

1996
Barack is elected to the Illinois State Senate.

1995
Barack's mother dies.

1992
Barack and Michelle are married.

1992
Barack begins teaching at the University of Chicago Law School.

August 2008
Barack is nominated as the Democratic candidate for the presidency.

February 10, 2007
Barack announces his candidacy for the office of president of the United States of America.

2006
Barack's second book, *The Audacity of Hope*, is published.

November 2004
Barack is elected to the U.S. Senate.

Michelle Obama, wife of President-elect Barack Obama, signals victory with two-thumbs up, as Barack, shown on the jumbo screen, acknowledges more than 240,000 people who have gathered in Grant Park, Chicago, Illinois, to celebrate on November 4, 2008.

Proclaiming Victory in Grant Park

Michelle Obama was stoked. After 21 months of hard campaigning, her husband Barack was about to be elected president. As the Obamas sat glued to the tube on that November night in 2008, watching the election returns come in, the drama was slowly building as Barack racked up state after state.

The Illinois senator was on a roll. Just after the polls closed, the TV networks started calling some big states for Barack—New York, New Jersey, and Massachusetts, among them. When Pennsylvania went for Barack, every heart in the room started thumping. When Ohio fell in Barack's column, Michelle knew victory was in their grasp.

Suddenly, the network commentator made it official: Barack had kicked it—crossing the magic threshold of 270 **electoral votes**. There was no way his opponent, Arizona Senator John McCain, could catch him now. The following January, Barack would be sworn in as the first African-American president in history. To Michelle, the future first lady, it all seemed like a dream. She said,

> **I remember we were watching the returns and, on one of the stations, Barack's picture came up and it said, 'President-elect Barack Obama.' And I looked at him and I said, 'You are the 44th president of the United States of America. Wow. What a country we live in.'**

VOTING AT SHOESMITH

For the Obamas, the day had started before dawn in the family home in Chicago's Hyde Park neighborhood. Michelle woke her daughters, Malia and Sasha, and got them ready for school. After breakfast, the Obamas hurried to Shoesmith Elementary School, where Barack and Michelle would vote. Arriving just after 7:30 A.M., the Obamas found hundreds of people waiting in a line that wrapped around the block. But the line immediately parted as the Obamas, accompanied by their children as well as aides, TV crews, and Secret Service agents, arrived at the school gym to cast their ballots.

Barack strode into the gym, wearing a wide grin, shaking hands and waving to friends and neighbors. It took the candidate just a few seconds to vote, but Michelle studied her ballot carefully. Later, Barack quipped that he wasn't sure Michelle had voted for him. He told reporters,

> **I had to check to see who she was voting for.**

After voting, the Obamas were issued receipts from local election officials, proving they had cast their ballots. Barack held his receipt high. News photographers snapped pictures of his gesture; later that day, the photos would find their way onto the pages of

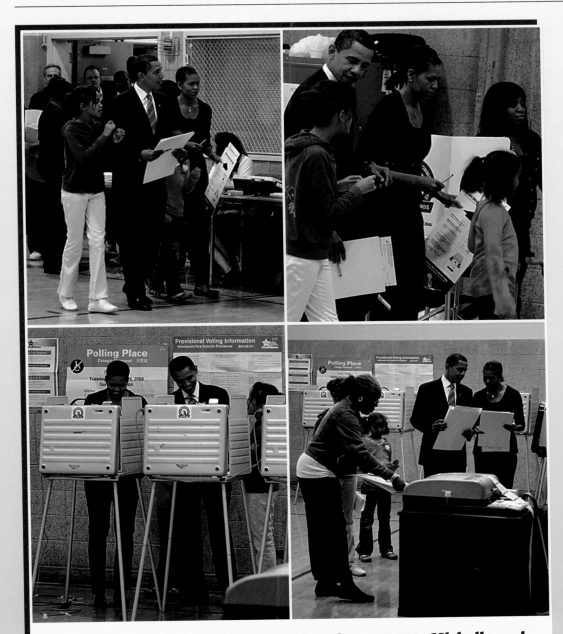

After breakfast on election day, November 4, 2008, Michelle and Barack Obama, accompanied by daughters Malia and Sasha, walk through the process and cast their votes at their neighborhood polling place—Shoesmith Elementary School on Chicago's South Side. Michelle took her time carefully reading and marking her ballot, whereas Barack completed his very quickly.

Avoiding an Embarrassing Moment

Michelle and Barack Obama voted at 7:36 A.M. at Shoesmith Elementary School in their Hyde Park neighborhood. Had they voted just a few minutes earlier, it is likely the Obamas would have encountered William Ayers at the polling place. Ayers, who also lives in Hyde Park, voted that morning but left the school just minutes before the Obamas arrived.

During the campaign, Barack was criticized by his opponent, Republican John McCain, for serving on a community board with Ayers. During the 1960s, Ayers was an active member of the Weather Underground, which committed acts of violence in protest of America's involvement in the Vietnam War. Barack insisted that he barely knew Ayers, who had long ago left his radical lifestyle behind and was now a college professor. Still, McCain suggested that Barack had shown poor judgment by associating with Ayers. During the campaign, McCain's running mate, Alaska Governor Sarah Palin, proclaimed that Barack couldn't be trusted because he was "pallin' around with terrorists."

Had Ayers still been voting when the Obamas arrived, it would have undoubtedly been an embarrassing moment for the candidate, who would have been caught on camera in the same room, and in close proximity, to a man whose reputation had caused Barack so much grief.

newspapers and be broadcast worldwide on TV and the Internet. As the Obamas left the Shoesmith gym, there was no denying that they had created electricity in the air; voters waiting to cast their ballots buzzed with excitement as the family left the building. One woman waiting in line to vote, 37-year-old Anna Cruz, told reporters,

❝ I'm really excited to be a part of this moment. History is being made. It's the first time a black candidate has made it this far and I believe he's going to win. ❞

After voting, Barack flew to Indiana for some last-minute campaigning before returning to Chicago for a family dinner. As for Michelle, she took the children to school, then returned home for a series of TV interviews that would be beamed by satellite to the so-called "battleground states"—the states where the vote count was sure to be tight. For the next several hours, Michelle sat at home, patiently answering questions posed to her by TV reporters based hundreds of miles away.

CELEBRATION IN GRANT PARK

As the Obamas sat in a hotel suite, watching the returns come in, the crowds started gathering in nearby Grant Park, where the Democrat planned to give a victory speech. By mid-morning, well before the polls closed, it was becoming clear that Barack was on

"Yes we can! Yes we can! Yes we can!" the crowd chanted, echoing a familiar Obama campaign slogan. Michelle was in awe, as more than 240,000 people assembled in Grant Park, Chicago, to celebrate Barack Obama being elected the 44th president of the United States. "Wow. What a country we live in," she exclaimed.

his way to defeating McCain. For months, Barack's message had found favor among the voters, who agreed with his commitment to end the Iraq War, breathe new life into a faltering economy, provide affordable health care to Americans, and return a sense of honor and mission to Washington.

During the final few days of campaigning, the public opinion polls had shown Barack holding leads in many of the states. On election day, voter turnout throughout the country had been awesome. Excitement was brewing throughout the country: people were flocking to the polls to vote for Barack Obama. Nowhere was that energy more evident than in Grant Park, where 240,000 people gathered to hear the first words uttered by the new president-elect.

Shortly after 10 P.M., the Obamas, accompanied by Malia and Sasha, left their hotel for the **motorcade** to Grant Park. As an international television audience of tens of millions tuned in, an announcer proclaimed, "Ladies and gentlemen, the next first family of the United States of America!" As soon as the Obamas walked onto the stage, the crowd erupted into cheers. Many started chanting the Obama campaign motto:

"Yes we can! Yes we can! Yes we can!"

One camera caught TV talk show host Oprah Winfrey, a long-time Obama supporter, leaning on the man in front of her, her eyes welling up in tears. Also caught weeping on camera was the Reverend Jesse Jackson, a longtime civil rights leader. Both African Americans, Winfrey and Jackson felt a deep sense of pride in how Barack had overcome decades of racism that had until now prevented a minority member from achieving the highest elected position in American government. Jackson's son, Congressman Jesse Jackson Jr., told a reporter,

"Tonight is an extraordinary celebration of an American story. Barack Obama has obviously engaged the American people."

CHICAGO

BREAKING NEWS

CNN HD **BARACK OBAMA ELECTED PRESIDENT**
AWAITING REMARKS BY JOHN MCCAIN

The Reverend Jesse Jackson was caught on camera, overwhelmed by emotion on this historic occasion. Jesse has been a civil rights activist all of his adult life, fighting racism and discrimination throughout America and the world, and he could hardly believe this day had come.

"ROCK OF OUR FAMILY"

Barack as well as Michelle, Sasha, and Malia strode onto the stage, waving to the crowd. Michelle wore a red and black dress that immediately caught the eyes of international fashion gurus, who hurried to track down the designer so they could render their opinions on the next first lady's sense of style. Throughout the campaign, Michelle had at times been praised by the snooty lords of the international fashion police for her choice in clothes; at other times her selections had been harshly dissed.

"Ladies and gentlemen, the next first family of the United States of America!" the announcer proclaimed, as Barack, Sasha, Malia, and Michelle calmly, confidently, and graciously walked onto the stage. Millions of people worldwide celebrated this extraordinary moment in American history. Michelle glowed; this was her day too.

After a few moments, Barack held up his hands to quiet the crowd. Michelle and the girls backed away, giving Barack the stage. Triumphantly, the president-elect addressed the crowd:

“I would not be standing here tonight without the unyielding support of my best friend for the last 16 years, the rock of our family and the love of my life, our nation's next first lady, Michelle Obama.”

About That Dress . . .

The red and black dress selected by Michelle Obama for the Grant Park victory celebration generally received a "thumbs down" from the nation's fashion gurus as well as people at home who participated in an online poll. Sixty-five percent of viewers who responded to an online poll conducted by *People* magazine said they "hated" the dress. And Jim Wetzel, owner of the trendy Jake Boutique of Chicago, said, "Not my favorite on her."

The dress was designed by New York fashion designer Narciso Rodriguez. The dress included a splash of red dots on a black front. Fashion writers heartily criticized the dress, finding that it made Michelle look frumpy and did not flatter her figure. Said *Los Angeles Times* fashion columnist Elizabeth Snead, "Such a historic night! Such an inspiring speech! And— sorry, but we have to say it—such a disastrous dress."

Michelle and the girls soon returned to join Barack on stage, along with Barack's running mate, U.S. Senator Joe Biden of Delaware and members of his family. On stage, the TV cameras caught Michelle and Barack in an embrace. Michelle leaned forward and spoke a few quiet words to her husband. Later, she said,

"I told him, 'Good job. Well done.' To walk out there and see thousands of hard-working folks, because so many people put their energy and their hopes into this campaign. To see the outcome and the emotion, it was a very emotional evening because I think people were ready to take hold of this country and help move it in a different direction, and you felt that."

Michelle Robinson wearing her cap and gown for her graduation photo from Princeton University in 1985. Michelle worked hard and was a good student, but growing up on Chicago's South Side, she also learned to be street smart.

2

Lawyer from the South Side

Michelle LaVaughn Robinson was tall and athletic, and she probably could have won a basketball **scholarship**, but that's not the path Michelle chose to take out of her tough South Side neighborhood in Chicago. Instead, she studied hard, made good grades, and was accepted to study at a prestigious **Ivy League** school.

But since Michelle was so smart, she had to watch herself on the streets. Her friends and classmates often had trouble in school and Michelle had to be careful not to make them feel jealous. Recalled Michelle,

> **"** What I learned growing up is that if I'm not going to get my butt kicked every day after school, I can't flaunt my intelligence in front of peers who are struggling with a whole range of things. You've got to be smart without acting smart. **"**

HITTING THE BOOKS

Michelle was born January 17, 1964, the younger of two children to Fraser Robinson III, a descendant of slaves from South Carolina, and his wife Marian. The Robinsons lived modestly in Chicago,

The Robinsons pose for a family portrait. Michelle, just an infant, is held by her mother, Marian, while her older brother Craig sits on his father, Fraser's lap. Fraser and Marian were a hard-working, middle-class couple who frequently reminded Michelle and her brother of the importance of getting a good education.

occupying a small apartment. Fraser, a pump operator for the city water department who died in 1990, suffered from multiple sclerosis, a disease that often left him weak and off balance. Still, he worked hard and his children adored him. Said Michelle's older brother Craig,

> **"We always felt like we couldn't let Dad down because he worked so hard for us. My sister and I, if one of us ever got in trouble with my father, we'd both be crying. We'd both be like, 'Oh, my god. Dad's upset. How could we do this to him?'"**

Craig was an awesome basketball player. A lot of big-time colleges were ready to hand him a scholarship, but Fraser told him that education was more important than basketball, so Craig accepted a partial scholarship to Princeton University in New Jersey. Princeton is one of the top colleges in America.

Trial By Basketball

Michelle Obama's brother, Craig Robinson, won a partial basketball scholarship to Princeton University. Following college, he was drafted by the Philadelphia 76ers. He didn't make it to the NBA, but he was good enough to play professionally in a European league before returning to the United States to coach college basketball at Oregon State University.

When Michelle first started dating Barack, Craig decided to judge his sister's new boyfriend on the court, so he challenged Barack to a one-on-one game. Barack had played on a high school team that won a state championship in Hawaii, but he was far less talented on the court than Craig. Still, Michelle's brother was impressed with Barack's moxie and will to win. Craig says,

> "Barack's game is just like his personality. He's confident, not afraid to shoot the ball when he's open. See, that says a lot about the guy. A lot of guys wanna just be out there to say they were out there. But he wants to be out there and be a part of the game."

Michelle was a good basketball player, too, but she also took Fraser's advice and hit the books, which helped her win a scholarship to Princeton University. After graduating from college, she earned another degree from Harvard University Law School in Boston, Massachusetts. And then she came back home to Chicago where she found a job at Sidley Austin, which is a big law firm in the city.

ICE CREAM AND A MOVIE

While working at Sidley Austin, Michelle met a young Harvard law student, Barack Obama, who had been hired for a summer job in 1989. It was her job to mentor Barack—essentially, she was his boss. Barack was immediately attracted to Michelle and soon asked for a date; at first she declined, believing it wrong for co-workers to see each other socially, but finally gave in. She said,

> **I thought, 'Oh, here you go. Here's this good-looking, smooth-talking guy. I've been down this road before.' Later, I was just shocked to find out that he really could communicate with people and he had some depth to him. He turned out to be an elite individual with strong moral values.**

On their first date, Barack and Michelle had ice cream, toured a museum, and saw director Spike Lee's movie *Do the Right Thing*, which tells the story of racial hatred on the streets of Brooklyn, New York. After that first summer, Barack returned to Harvard to finish school, but Michelle and Barack kept in touch and saw each other often.

Michelle left Sidley Austin in 1991 to take a job on the staff of Chicago Mayor Richard M. Daley. By now, Barack and Michelle were engaged, and Barack was concerned that Michelle would be swallowed up by the rough and tumble world of Chicago politics.

Michelle and Barack share the Christmas holiday early in their relationship. At first Michelle said "no" when Barack asked her out on a date, because she was his boss. However, Barack's persistence eventually paid off, when Michelle finally said "yes" and went out with Barack, and their romance began.

Before accepting the job, Michelle, Barack, and Daley's chief of staff, Valerie Jarrett, met for lunch. "My fiancé wants to know who is going to be looking out for me and making sure I thrive," Michelle told Jarrett. Valerie Jarrett assured Barack that she would personally keep an eye on Michelle and shield her from politics. At the end of the meal, Jarrett asked Barack, "Well, did I pass the test?" Barack assured Jarrett that she did, and Michelle agreed to work for Daley.

The Daleys of Chicago

No family has dominated politics in the Illinois city of Chicago as much as the Daleys. Born in 1902, Richard J. Daley served as mayor of Chicago from 1955 until his death in 1972. During his administration, he was the undisputed boss of city politics, wielding enormous influence over the Chicago Democratic "machine." In 1960, his strong support for John F. Kennedy helped the Massachusetts senator win the state of Illinois in the presidential race, which in turn helped swing the national election to Kennedy.

His son, Richard M. Daley, has been mayor since 1989. He is not regarded as the old-style big city boss in the mold of his father, but Mayor Daley is still a powerful figure in Illinois politics. In early 2007, he was one of the first major politicians in America to endorse Barack Obama for the presidency.

GRITTY WORK

The meeting paid dividends for everyone—Michelle got the job, Barack (who by now was harboring political ambitions), was able to make some important contacts in the mayor's office, and Jarrett met somebody whose star was just starting to rise. Eventually, Jarrett became a close advisor to Barack as he made an impact in the world of Chicago politics.

Michelle worked for Daley until 1993, then left to establish Public Allies, a nonprofit agency that seeks jobs for students.

Michelle and Barack in a relaxed moment on their wedding day, 1992.

Under the program, students work in homeless shelters, city offices, and other places where they can help people. For Michelle, it was the type of gritty, public service work she truly enjoyed. As for Michelle and Barack, their romance continued and in 1992 they married.

Michelle, a devoted mother, holds younger daughter Sasha, while Barack holds older daughter, Malia, as the family poses for a photo, 2002. For Michelle and Barack, maintaining a close and caring family unit is a very high priority.

3

Devoted Mother, Vigorous Campaigner

When Barack told Michelle that he hoped to enter politics, she was at first supportive. Michelle could see an intensity in her new husband: he had a tremendous desire to help others and a deep sense of empathy for less fortunate people. Michelle was also astounded by Barack's energy. He always seemed to be in motion.

After graduating from law school Barack took a job organizing a voter registration drive in Illinois, then joined a Chicago law firm. At night, he taught at the University of Chicago's law school. After class, Barack would spend several hours working on his first book, *Dreams from My Father*, which told the story of his African heritage. Michelle couldn't see how Barack could fit politics into

Michelle and Barack in Kenya, Africa, 1992. Barack was working on writing his first book, *Dreams from My Father—A Story of Race and Inheritance*, and the young couple visited Kenya, Barack's father's home country, to learn more about his father's family and the place where they lived.

all that, but she told him if he wanted to run for office she would stand behind him. She recalled,

> **❝I told him, 'If that's what you really want to do, I think you'd be great at it. You are everything people say they want in their public officials.'❞**

FEARS COMING TRUE

Soon after their wedding, Michelle and Barack made their new home on the South Side. Michelle continued to work for Public

Allies, but in 1996 she joined the University of Chicago for the first in a series of administrative positions. Eventually, she took over the Office of Community and External Affairs at the University of Chicago Hospitals, where she found herself with the sensitive job of turning poor, uninsured people away from the emergency room. These patients were not in need of emergency care, they simply had no other place to go for routine medical needs. Working with the patients, Michelle was able to find them family doctors who could better serve their needs while saving the hospital the expense of treating people in the emergency room.

The Obamas' first daughter, Malia, was born in 1998; younger daughter Natasha, whom the Obamas call Sasha, followed in 2001. Meanwhile, Barack's political career had commenced; in 1996, he won his first election to a seat in the state Senate. Soon, Michelle realized the fears she first had about her husband were coming true—now that he was in politics, he had little time for his family. With his job taking him to the state capital in Springfield and his spare time dominated by his constituents, Barack was clearly neglecting Michelle, Malia, and Sasha.

And so Michelle made it clear to Barack that he would have to slow down his career so he could devote time to his young family. Barack consented and eventually took some flack when he missed a vote in Springfield on an important gun control measure known as the Safe Neighborhoods program after refusing to cut short a family vacation in Hawaii. Malia was ill at the time, and Barack refused to leave her—even though his absence from the capital helped kill the program. Later, he told reporters,

"I cannot sacrifice the health or well-being of my daughter for politics. I had to make a decision based on what I felt was appropriate for my daughter and for my wife. If the press takes my absence as the reason for the failure of the Safe Neighborhoods bill, then that's how the press is going to report it."

BEHIND THE SCENES PLAYER

In 1999, Barack made his first run for office in Washington, losing an election for the U.S. House. After the loss, he returned to the state senate where he emerged as a major force in state politics. In 2004, Barack entered the race for the U.S. Senate, easily defeating the Republican candidate, conservative **pundit** Alan Keyes. During that race, Michelle proved herself to be a vigorous campaigner. On a campaign visit to a tough Chicago neighborhood, Michelle waded into a crowd of thugs who threatened to disrupt the event, ordering them to leave. Ron Carter, publisher of an African-American weekly newspaper in Chicago, saw the incident. He recalled,

> **There were lots of radicals protesting, calling into question [Barack's] loyalty to the community. She came out the back door, and there were a bunch of hoodlum thugs ready to do a full-blast demonstration. She put on her street sense and asked all the guys, 'Y'all got a problem or something?' They all froze, guys who would slap the mayor, who would slap Jesse Jackson in the face, even.**

After entering the race for the U.S. Senate, Barack came to the attention of presidential candidate John Kerry, who offered him the opportunity to make the **keynote address** at the 2004 Democratic National Convention in Boston in July. Barack's fiery and dramatic rhetoric made him the star of the convention as he called for Americans to bury their differences and unite for a common cause.

Kerry would go on to lose the election to President George W. Bush, but Democrats couldn't help but be dazzled by the rising star who delivered their keynote address. The most vigorous applause was heard as Barack told the audience,

> **Now even as we speak, there are those who are preparing to divide us, the spin masters and negative ad peddlers who embrace the politics of anything goes. . . .**

Michelle, Barack, Malia, and Sasha have reason to smile as they are covered by an avalanche of confetti after Barack, who had just been elected Senator from Illinois, delivered his acceptance speech in Chicago, November 2, 2004.

Well, I say to them tonight, there's not a liberal America and a conservative America; there's the United States of America. . . . There's not a black America and white America and Latino America and Asian America; there's the United States of America. **"**

Behind the scenes, Michelle worked closely with Barack on the speech. It was Michelle who recognized that if her husband made a successful speech, he would boost his profile as a nationally prominent political figure. Seconds before he walked onto the stage to deliver the speech, Michelle told him, "Just don't screw it up, buddy."

Michelle stands by her husband's side in front of the Old State Capitol Building in Springfield, Illinois, as Senator Barack Obama officially announces his candidacy for the presidency, February 10, 2007.

The Presidential Campaign Begins

On the bitterly cold day of February 10, 2007, Barack took the stage in front of the Old State Capitol in Springfield, Illinois. As the thermometer hovered around 16 degrees, the senator surveyed the huge crowd in front of him. He grinned and said, "I know it's a little chilly, but I'm fired up."

More than 16,000 people in the crowd cheered. Michelle and the girls stood on the stage as well, shivering with everyone else on that blustery day. Soon, though, most folks forgot the cold as Barack announced his intentions to seek the presidency in 2008.

While Barack talked about his vision to unite America and solve some of the country's enormous problems, many saw the historical significance of electing the first African-American candidate to the presidency. As for Michelle, she was thinking in more practical terms. The election for president was 22 months away. Michelle could see a long campaign ahead, fought against some formidable opponents, including Senator Hillary Clinton, as Barack vied for the Democratic **nomination** and then the presidency in the general election. Later, she said,

> ❝We've got to win a bunch of states and delegates and, you know, this is a messy process. And then there's still a general election. So I am far away from history right now. Why get caught up . . . emotionally when there's so much stuff in front of us that we have to do?❞

The Old State Capitol

The site in Springfield, Illinois, where Barack Obama chose to open his candidacy for the presidency holds a special place in American history. In 1858, Abraham Lincoln launched his unsuccessful candidacy for the U.S. Senate against Stephen Douglas in front of what is now known as the Old State Capitol. As the nation inched slowly toward civil war, Lincoln warned Americans, "A house divided against itself cannot stand."

One hundred fifty years later, Barack stood in front of the Old State Capitol and told a crowd of supporters,

"We can build a more hopeful America. And that is why, in the shadow of the Old State Capitol, where Lincoln once called for a house divided to stand together, where common hopes and common dreams still live, I stand before you today to announce my candidacy for presidency of the United States of America."

COMING ON BOARD

Michelle was one of the last to come on board for the campaign. She knew her husband had ambitions, but by now the Obamas had settled into comfortable and prosperous careers. Barack entered

Michelle and Barack are featured on the February 15, 2005 cover of *SaVoy*, an upscale African-American lifestyle magazine. There could be no doubt that Barack and Michelle were each rising stars in their own rights, and together, an unstoppable force.

the Senate in early 2005, establishing himself as one of the brightest young lawmakers in Washington. In just two years in the Senate, Barack had already written some important **legislation**, including a law to provide better health care and other benefits to wounded veterans of the Iraq and Afghanistan wars, as well as a law that made most of the federal **budget** accessible on the Internet. Meanwhile, he found the time to write a second book, *The Audacity of Hope*, which expanded on the vision of unity he first raised in his 2004 keynote address to the Democratic convention.

Both of Barack's books were bestsellers, enabling the Obamas to afford a $1.6 million home in Hyde Park. Michelle was also doing well: she was now a vice president of the University of Chicago Hospitals, earning a salary of nearly $300,000 a year.

But with the wars continuing in Afghanistan and Iraq and with the economy faltering, Barack made the decision to seek the presidency. Michelle knew that a campaign for national office could evolve into a long and grueling life for the family, but that wasn't her main concern. Rather, a large measure of Michelle's hesitancy centered on the nature of elective politics in America: she feared that the family would be dragged through the mud by Barack's rivals. And she also feared for her husband, fretting that somebody harboring racist notions would make an attempt on his life. In fact, soon after Barack announced his candidacy the Secret Service assigned a detail of agents to protect him. In the end, though, Michelle decided to put her fears aside. She said,

> **❝ The realities are that as a black man Barack can get shot going to the gas station, you know, so . . . you can't make a decision based on fear and the possibility of what might happen. We just weren't raised that way. ❞**

THROWING HERSELF INTO CAMPAIGNING

Soon after Barack won the 2004 Senate election, the Obamas decided not to move as a family to Washington. Barack and Michelle wanted Sasha and Malia to continue attending their school in Chicago. Michelle also wanted to keep her job at the University of Chicago Hospitals. And so Barack went to Washington without his family, taking a small apartment near Capitol Hill but returning on weekends to Hyde Park. The arrangement helped Michelle and the girls lead something of a normal life while Barack remained the focus of attention in the nation's capital.

But as Barack's presidential campaign started unfolding, it meant that Michelle would have to take an active part in his political career. She responded with enthusiasm, throwing herself into campaigning for Barack as vigorously as she had in the 2004 Senate election.

Michelle introduces her husband, U.S. Senator and Democratic presidential hopeful, Barack Obama, at a fundraiser in New York City, March 9, 2007. Michelle became Barack's biggest fan and most vocal advocate, campaigning tirelessly for him all across the country.

Michelle (center, signing a placard) is surrounded by enthusiastic supporters at a "Women for Obama '08" event in Las Vegas, June 13, 2007. This is Michelle's first stop in the state of Nevada on behalf of her husband since the Illinois senator launched his presidential campaign, and the turnout is extraordinary.

She soon found herself visiting dozens of cities, speaking to small groups and large crowds. Journalists interviewed her. The days were long and the travel tedious, but there were many light moments in the campaign, such as when she confided to news reporters that her husband snores at night and suffers from bad breath in the morning. During one campaign appearance, Michelle jived about all the fuss people made about her husband. She said,

❝ This Barack Obama guy's pretty impressive. . . . Then, there's the Barack Obama that lives in my house. That guy's not impressive. He still has trouble . . . putting his

socks actually in the dirty clothes and he still doesn't do a better job than our 5-year-old daughter Sasha making his bed. So you have to forgive me if I'm a little stunned by this whole Barack Obama thing. **"**

A REAL AND LEGITIMATE CHANCE

Certainly, Michelle was proving herself to be an asset to Barack's campaign. There is no question that as Barack started campaigning he faced a measure of racism. In the past, many white Americans had not been comfortable with the notion of voting for an African American for national office, but here were Barack and Michelle, both successful Harvard University–educated lawyers, showing that African Americans were capable of achieving great things.

African-American Candidates

Barack Obama was not the first African-American candidate to seek national office. In 1872, the former slave and civil rights leader, Frederick Douglass, sought the vice presidency as the candidate of the Equal Rights Party. Douglass and his running mate, presidential candidate Victoria Woodhull, ultimately received few votes.

The first African-American candidate to seek the presidential nomination of a major party was Shirley Chisholm, a congresswoman from New York, who competed in several Democratic primaries in 1968. The first African-American candidate to win a primary was Rev. Jesse Jackson, who won five Democratic primaries and caucuses in the 1984 contest. Four years later, Jackson competed again and this time won 13 primaries and caucuses.

Others who sought the presidency were Carol Moseley Braun, a senator from Illinois; Alan Keyes, who staged a brief candidacy for the presidency before opposing Barack in the 2004 Senate race; Leonora Fulani, a social activist who ran as an independent in 1988 and 1992; and Rev. Al Sharpton, a civil rights leader who campaigned for the Democratic nomination in 2004. All those campaigns fell short, but each helped pry the door open a little bit more, enabling an African-American candidate to be regarded as a serious contender for the nation's highest office.

Michelle helped ease the fears of many whites about voting for a black candidate; she also helped raise enthusiasm in the African-American community, as she sent the message that, this time, an African American had a real and legitimate chance of winning the **White House**. Later, Michelle appeared on the hit TV talk show *The View*. One of the show's panelists, African-American comedienne Whoopi Goldberg, told her,

> **Any time you see black folks on the news, particularly women, they have no teeth, and the teeth that they have have gold around them and they can't put a sentence together. You're helping change a perception. I know that sounds funny and silly. . . . I just want to say thanks.**

COMMITMENT TO THE GIRLS

Barack's presidential campaign had changed life for the Obama family. Michelle had to step back from her own career, taking a leave of absence from her job. Meanwhile, she still tried to be as much of a full-time mom as possible, although she often had to call on her mother or friends and neighbors to make sure Malia and Sasha got to school, made it to their after-school activities, and were put to bed on time. Michelle made the commitment to the girls, though, that she would not spend more than one night at a time away from home. At one point, she confided to friends that she felt torn between her responsibilities to the campaign and to her daughters. She said,

> **When I'm at work [on the campaign] I'm guilty because I am not with my girls and when I'm with my girls, I'm thinking I should be doing more to help the campaign.**

Still, there was a lot of excitement on the campaign trail. Barack was consistently drawing big crowds to his campaign events. He

Michelle talks to her daughters Malia and Sasha behind the stage as U.S. Senator Barack Obama speaks at a campaign event at Iowa State University in Ames, Iowa, on February 11, 2007. Michelle and Barack work to include the girls in the campaign activities, while keeping their lives as normal as possible.

soon found himself appearing on the covers of national magazines and interviewed by network TV anchors. Michelle was drawing some big crowds, too. Early in the year, Michelle and Barack split up the campaign duties. It made more sense for them to campaign separately—that way they could reach more people. As the year went on, Michelle started feeling more and more confident that Barack could win this thing. In an interview with a reporter, Michelle said,

Michelle waves to supporters at a campaign rally for Barack at the Hy-Vee Conference Center in Des Moines, Iowa, on December 8, 2007. Iowa held the first-in-the-nation caucuses for the 2008 presidential election on January 3, 2008, and therefore the Iowa caucuses become very important for each candidate.

" To me, it's now or never. We're not going to keep running and running and running, because at some point you do get the life beaten out of you. It hasn't been beaten out of us yet. We need to be in there now, while we're still fresh and open and fearless and bold . . .

So if we're going to be cautious, I'd rather let somebody else do it. . . . If we're going to uproot our lives, then let's hopefully make a real big dent in what it means to be president of the United States. **"**

Despite all their optimism and hard work, though, by late December the public opinion polls still showed Barack well behind the front-runner, Senator Hillary Rodham Clinton of New York, who maintained a commanding lead of 29 points over Barack. But as Barack marshaled his campaign team at the end of 2007 and planned his strategy for the long run, the election was about to take a dramatic turn.

Hillary Rodham Clinton

Barack Obama's chief rival for the Democratic nomination for president in 2007 and 2008 was U.S. Senator Hillary Rodham Clinton of New York, the wife of former president Bill Clinton. As first lady, Hillary Clinton opened many doors for women in politics—more of an advisor than a hostess, Clinton often helped her husband craft policy.

In 1993 and 1994, President Clinton put her in charge of his effort to reform the nation's health care system, but the effort failed due to stiff opposition from political leaders who believed that under Clinton's plan, the government would become too influential in deciding how health care is delivered. In 2000, Hillary Clinton ran for the U.S. Senate representing New York State. She won the election, and soon emerged as a candidate for the 2008 presidential nomination. Although Clinton lost the nomination, Barack recognized her intelligence and savvy and soon after winning election as president appointed her secretary of state.

The Obama family celebrates after Barack wins the 2008 Iowa Caucus in Des Moines, Iowa, January 3, 2008. Barack's message appealed to the working-class people of Iowa, and his win came as quite a surprise to Hillary Rodham Clinton, who up to that point in time had been leading in the polls.

5

Preparing for 1600 Pennsylvania Avenue

When Michelle arrived in Iowa in late 2007 to campaign, she wondered whether Barack would survive this early test of his candidacy. Iowa was the first state to **caucus** in the presidential race, meaning it would be the first time the candidates for president faced the voters. After all, weeks before the Iowa caucuses the polls showed Barack trailing Senator Clinton.

Iowa is mostly a farm state. There are few cities in Iowa, which means few concentrations of African-American voters. Certainly, to win the presidential contest, Barack would have to appeal to voters of all races. But Michelle and others close to the campaign knew that black voters were vital to Barack's chances because they could be expected to make him competitive with the other candidates in what promised to be a tight race. And so, as Michelle visited the rural towns of Iowa she couldn't help but think to herself, "Ain't no black people in Iowa."

Michelle's fears were soon put to rest. Barack was able to call on strong support from young voters as well as an effective organization of volunteers who made sure his supporters got to the caucus sites. On January 3, 2008, voters in Iowa met in high school gyms, church rec halls, and similar places to caucus and cast their ballots for the Democratic and Republican nominations. Barack's team turned out in full force, helping shepherd Obama voters into groups and making sure they stuck together at the caucus sites, fending off invitations from other candidates. When the caucusing in Iowa concluded, Democrats gave Barack a strong victory over Senator Clinton, establishing him as one of the front-runners for the nomination.

SHIFT IN MOMENTUM

Clinton recovered a few days later to win the New Hampshire **primary**, but by mid-February momentum was clearly on Barack's side. However, while running off an impressive string of 12 straight caucus and primary wins, the campaign suffered one of its few stumbles when Michelle made something of a verbal **gaffe** on the campaign trail. Speaking in Wisconsin, Michelle told an audience that her husband's victories showed that Americans were anxious for change. She said,

> **For the first time in my adult lifetime, I am really proud of my country, and not just because Barack has done well, but because I think people are hungry for change.**

Political opponents immediately jumped on those remarks, questioning Michelle's patriotism. Among the most vocal critics were conservative TV pundit Bill O'Reilly, who said, "I don't want to go on a lynching party against Michelle Obama unless there's evidence, hard facts, that says this is how the woman really feels." And Cindy McCain, the wife of Republican presidential candidate John McCain, huffed, "I don't know about you, if you heard those words earlier, I'm very proud of my country." As for Michelle, she shrugged off the criticism, telling a reporter,

> **"I have not paid much attention about what people say about me who don't know me. It would be very hard for me to function in this world and to go through Princeton and Harvard and to work in all the careers that I've worked if I worried about labels."**

Michelle speaks to the crowd at the "Stand For Change Rally" in Houston, Texas, March 3, 2008. After trailing Senator Hillary Clinton in the polls for many months, the tide had turned and Barack's campaign was surging ahead. Michelle and Barack crisscrossed the country, spreading their message of hope, unity, and change.

Not many voters seemed to agree with O'Reilly and Cindy McCain. By late spring, Barack found himself well in the lead for the Democratic nomination but Clinton continued to remain competitive. Finally, during the last round of primaries in early June, Barack scored enough **delegates** to guarantee the nomination. On the night of June 3, at a rally in Minneapolis, Minnesota, Michelle introduced her husband so that he could make a speech claiming the nomination. Just before Michelle turned to leave the stage, she exchanged a brief bump of the fists with Barack. It was an innocent, comical, and touching gesture, but one conservative pundit, Fox News commentator E.D. Hill, let loose with some rage, wondering out loud whether it was in reality a "terrorist fist jab."

Michelle bumps fists with Barack at a rally in St. Paul, Minnesota, June 3, 2008. A Fox News Channel report depicted the fist bump as a "terrorist fist jab." Michelle later explained that she learned the greeting from young staffers on the Obama campaign. "It's the new high-five," she said.

Michelle (3rd from left) made her debut appearance on ABC's "The View," fist bumping the co-hosts, June 18, 2008. Michelle also set a fashion trend while she was on the show. The $148 off-the-rack Donna Ricco dress she wore on the show flew off the racks, selling out at most of the clothing chain's 322 retail stores all across the country within days of her appearance.

THE CAMPAIGN TURNS UGLY

Hill took a lot of grief for that comment and, a few days later, broadcast an apology to the Obamas. She said, "I certainly didn't mean to associate the word 'terrorist' in any way to Senator Obama and his wife."

Although Hill was forced to take back her words, there is no question that Michelle's fears about the campaign turning ugly were coming true. And not all of the attacks were aimed at Barack—some were aimed at Michelle. Just before she visited Nashville, Tennessee, on a campaign swing, the Tennessee Republican Party posted a video on the Internet of her Wisconsin speech, adding in a news release,

"**The Tennessee Republican Party has always been proud of America. To further honor the occasion of Mrs. Obama's visit, the Tennessee Republican Party has requested the playing of patriotic music by radio stations across the state.**"

Meanwhile, as the Democratic convention neared in late summer, the *New Yorker* magazine featured a cartoon of Michelle and Barack on the cover in which Michelle was drawn as a 1960s-style radical bumping fists with Barack who was depicted as an Islamic terrorist. The Obama campaign immediately issued a statement suggesting the cartoon was in poor taste, but the *New Yorker*'s editors stood by the cover, insisting that it was intended as a spoof and that its real intent was to show how the Obamas' critics were guilty of making outlandish and ridiculous claims.

Sudoku and Will Smith

Michelle Obama rises at 4 A.M. every morning to exercise on a treadmill in the Obama family home. In her spare time, she does sudoku puzzles, which are math puzzles that require the solver to line up numbers 1 through 9 in nine rows without repeating any of the numbers.

Michelle's favorite foods are dark chocolate, macaroni and cheese, and French fries. She enjoys baking shortbread cookies, listening to music by Stevie Wonder, and reading books by Toni Morrison, who writes novels about the African-American experience in America.

Michelle also enjoys comedy. Her favorite TV shows include *Sex in the City*, a comedy chronicling the lives of single women in New York, as well as reruns of the old *Dick Van Dyke Show*, a 1960s-era sitcom about the antics of a TV comedy writer. One of Michelle's favorite films is *Enchanted*, a musical about storybook characters who find themselves magically transplanted to New York. And, finally, Michelle loves anything starring Will Smith.

Michelle speaks to thousands of attendees at the Democratic National Convention at the Pepsi Center in Denver, Colorado, and millions of television viewers around the country and the world, August 25, 2008. Her message was of the importance of family, dignity, integrity, and mutual respect.

In late August, the Democratic National Convention convened in Denver to reward Barack with the official nomination of the party. Michelle had a big role at the convention, delivering an important speech on the first night of the event. During her speech she concentrated on the strong ties that keep the Obama family together, telling the delegates:

> **❝ What struck me when I first met Barack was that even though he had this funny name, even though he'd grown up all the way across the continent in Hawaii,**

his family was so much like mine. He was raised by grandparents who were working-class folks just like my parents, and by a single mother who struggled to pay the bills just like we did. Like my family, they scrimped and saved so that he could have opportunities they never had themselves.

And Barack and I were raised with so many of the same values: that you work hard for what you want in life; that your word is your bond and you do what you say you're going to do; that you treat people with dignity and respect, even if you don't know them, and even if you don't agree with them. **"**

ADVOCATE FOR MOTHERS

Barack left Denver with a big lead in the polls over his opponent, John McCain and, by the fall, it was clear that the Republican would never be able to close the gap. Except for a few days following the Republican convention, McCain consistently trailed Barack in the polls and, on election day, the senator from Illinois scored an impressive victory.

Michelle and Barack celebrated Barack's extraordinary victory on election night in Grant Park, Chicago, with 240,000 enthusiastic supporters. Immediately after the election, Barack got down to work planning his new administration and preparing for his inauguration in January. He selected members of his cabinet as well as other important officials who would help him administer the federal government.

Michelle had many details to look after as well. She had to make plans to move the family to Washington and find a new school for Malia and Sasha. After touring several schools in the Washington area, Michelle picked Sidwell Friends, an exclusive private school that has educated the children of many prominent Washington families, including Chelsea Clinton, the daughter of President Bill Clinton, and Julie and Tricia Nixon, the daughters of President Richard M. Nixon.

First lady Laura Bush (left) and Michelle, the soon-to-be first lady, meet in the private residence of the White House in Washington, D.C. on November 10, 2008, less than one week after Barack was elected president.

Just a few days after the election, the Obamas were invited to the White House by President Bush and his wife, Laura, the first lady. While Barack met with the president to discuss the transition of power, Laura Bush gave Michelle a tour of the White House.

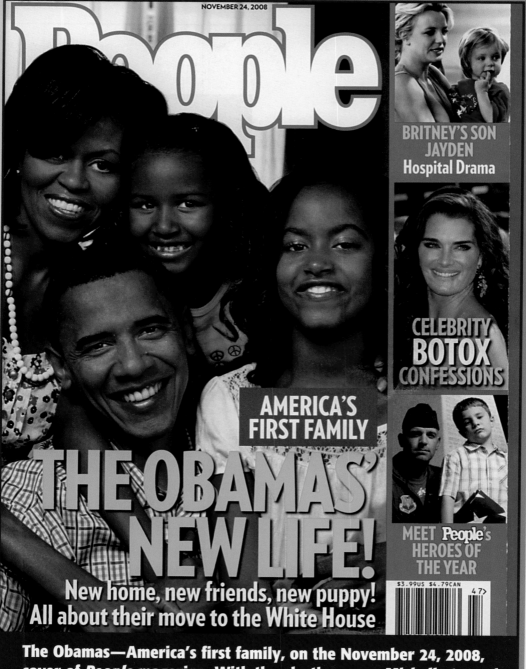

NOVEMBER 24, 2008

People

BRITNEY'S SON JAYDEN Hospital Drama

CELEBRITY BOTOX CONFESSIONS

MEET *People's* **HEROES OF THE YEAR**

$3.99US $4.79CAN

47>

AMERICA'S FIRST FAMILY

THE OBAMAS' NEW LIFE!

New home, new friends, new puppy! All about their move to the White House

The Obamas—America's first family, on the November 24, 2008, cover of *People* magazine. With the election over, Michelle turned her attention to settling the family into their new home—the White House, and preparing to serve as America's first lady.

The Obama Kids

Malia Obama plays soccer and enjoys dance and drama. She also enjoys reading the *Harry Potter* books, and so do her mom and dad. Now, Barack and Malia are both reading the books in the *Twilight* series, which are romantic stories about a teenage girl who falls in love with a vampire.

Sasha Obama is interested in gymnastics and tap dance. Both girls take lessons in piano and tennis. Both girls are also considered excellent ping-pong players. Throughout the campaign, Barack and Michelle made commitments to be devoted parents. Michelle refused to do any traveling that kept her away from the girls for more than a single night. The girls' grandmother, Marian Robinson, usually pitched in to watch the girls in her absence. Meanwhile, on the day following his election as president, Barack attended a parent-teacher conference at his girls' school.

As the Obamas settle into life at 1600 Pennsylvania Avenue, Michelle sees a lot of challenges ahead as the nation's newest first lady. In addition to serving as White House hostess, where she will be responsible for greeting the hundreds of dignitaries who meet with Barack each year, Michelle plans to become an advocate for the needs of single and working mothers—the type of people she knew as she grew up on Chicago's South Side. She said,

"These issues are my passions. Now that the election is won, I'll keep working to find solutions that make a real difference in people's lives. With Barack serving as president, we will fill our home with talk of how to serve our nation's families better."

1964   Michelle LaVaughn Robinson is born in Chicago on January 17.

1981   Graduates from Whitney Young High School in Chicago and enrolls at Princeton University in New Jersey.

1985   Graduates from Princeton and enrolls at Harvard University School of Law in Massachusetts.

1988   Graduates from Harvard and joins Sidley Austin, a Chicago law firm, as an associate.

1989   Meets and starts dating Barack Obama, a young law student she mentors for the summer at Sidley Austin.

1991   Joins the staff of Chicago Mayor Richard M. Daley as an aide.

1992   Marries Barack.

1993   Accepts a job as executive director of Public Allies, a nonprofit organization that finds jobs for students.

1996   Joins the University of Chicago as associate dean of student services; Barack wins his first political race, a seat in the Illinois State Senate.

1998   Daughter Malia is born.

2001   Daughter Sasha is born.

2002   Named director of community affairs for the University of Chicago Hospitals.

2004   Campaigns for Barack to win a U.S. Senate seat; works closely with Barack on his keynote address for the Democratic National Convention in Denver, Colorado.

2005   Named vice president for community and external affairs for the University of Chicago Hospitals.

2007   Takes a leave of absence from her job to campaign full time for Barack, who runs for president.

2008   Barack Obama is elected 44th president of the United States.

2009   The Obamas move into the White House.

1975 Selected as the sixth-grade class salutatorian at Bouchet Elementary School in Chicago.

1981 Selected for membership to the National Honor Society and elected senior class treasurer at Whitney Young High School in Chicago.

1985 Graduated cum laude from Princeton University in New Jersey.

1988 Graduated with a law degree from Harvard University in Massachusetts.

2006 Named by *Essence* magazine to its list of "25 of the World's Most Inspiring Women."

Named a "Young 'Un," one of 26 influential young African-American women, by Oprah Winfrey at the TV talk show host's Legends Ball.

Serves as a board member for the Chicago Council on Global Affairs and University of Chicago Laboratory Schools.

2007 Named to the list of "10 of the World's Best Dressed People" by *Vanity Fair* magazine.

Selected by *02138* magazine as a member of the "Harvard 100," a list of the year's most influential Harvard University alumni.

Serves as a board member for the Chicago Council on Global Affairs and University of Chicago Laboratory Schools.

2008 Named to *People* magazine's list of "10 Best-Dressed Women."

Selected for an honorary membership to the Princeton University chapter of Alpha Kappa Alpha, the nation's 100-year-old black sorority.

Named to the list of "10 of the World's Best Dressed People" by *Vanity Fair* magazine.

Serves as a board member for the Chicago Council on Global Affairs and University of Chicago Laboratory Schools.

budget—In government, the document that is developed before the start of the year specifying exactly how much money the government plans to spend during the following year.

caucus—Process used by some states to award delegates to presidential candidates; in a caucus, voters meet in groups and cast their ballots in public, often by a show of hands.

delegates—Officials of the Republican and Democratic parties selected through primaries and caucuses and designated to cast votes to nominate presidential candidates at the party conventions.

electoral votes—The official votes cast by the Electoral College in the presidential election that reflect the popular votes in the states.

gaffe—Something said or done that is socially upsetting or incorrect.

Ivy League—Officially, a sports league made up of eight of the top colleges in America, but the term is commonly used to refer to the academic reputations of the schools, which get their name from the ivy that covers the walls of the schools' old buildings.

keynote address—The major speech delivered at the opening of the national political conventions, or similar events, intended to set the tone for the conventions and inspire the delegates.

legislation—Actions by bodies of lawmakers to develop new laws.

motorcade—Long line of cars, often led and trailed by police vehicles, used to transport a head of state or other dignitary over city streets or highways.

nomination—The designation awarded by the Republican and Democratic parties to the candidates who win majorities of the delegates during the primaries and caucuses.

primary—Process used by many states to award delegates to presidential candidates.

pundit—Writer or broadcaster who offers opinions on political issues.

scholarship—Financial assistance offered by a school or college to help a student pay the cost of tuition.

White House—Official residence of the president and first family in Washington; the address of the White House is 1600 Pennsylvania Avenue.

Books and Periodicals

Brophy, David Bergen. *Michelle Obama: Meet the First Lady*. New York: HarperCollins, 2009.

Colbert, David. *Michelle Obama: An American Story*. Boston: Sandpiper, 2008.

Collins, Lauren. "The Other Obama," *New Yorker* (March 10, 2008): p. 88.

Davis, William Michael. *Barack Obama: The Politics of Hope*. Stockton, N.J.: OTTN Publishing, 2008.

Mendell, David. *Obama: From Promise to Power*. New York: Amistad, 2007.

Mundy, Liza. *Michelle: A Biography*. New York: Simon & Schuster, 2008.

Obama, Barack. *Dreams from My Father: A Story of Race and Inheritance*. New York: Crown, 2004.

Paulson, Amanda. "Michelle Obama's Story," *Christian Science Monitor* (August 25, 2008): p. 1.

Web Sites

www.barackobama.com

Obama for America, the campaign committee that worked to elect Barack Obama to the presidency, maintains a Web site that explains the issues the 44th president must tackle during his administration. Students can find biographies of Barack and Michelle and read copies of some of Barack's major speeches.

www.illinoishistory.gov/hs/old_capitol.htm

The Illinois Historic Preservation Agency maintains a Web site dedicated to the Old State Capitol, the place where Abraham Lincoln delivered his "House Divided" speech, and also the place where Barack Obama announced his candidacy for the presidency. Students can read a history of the historic building and take a virtual tour.

www.princeton.edu

Web site for Princeton University, the college attended by Michelle Obama as an undergraduate. Students can read about life on campus, university projects, the Princeton athletic teams and the creative and performing arts at the school.

www.whitehouse.gov

Official Web site of the White House chronicles the activities of the first family and provides information on many key issues addressed by the president. Students can find biographies of all presidents and first ladies on the site, learn about the history of the executive mansion and take an interactive tour.

page

ABOUT THE AUTHOR

Hal Marcovitz is a former newspaper reporter who has written more than 100 books for young readers. In 2005, *Nancy Pelosi*, his biography of House Speaker Nancy Pelosi, was named to *Booklist* magazine's list of recommended feminist books for young readers. He lives in Chalfont, Pennsylvania, with his wife Gail and daughter Ashley.